D1566357

MS. BARTLETT'S
FAMILIAR QUOTATIONS

MS. BARTLETT'S
FAMILIAR QUOTATIONS

Jane Bartlett

JOSEPH TABLER
SAN DIEGO

Published by Joseph Tabler - Books
3817 5th Avenue, San Diego, CA 92103
Copyright © 1978, 1983, 1991
Printed and bound in the United States of America

First Paperback edition, first printing 1991

Library of Congress Catalog Number: 91-66093

ISBN 0-9610330-4-5

CONTENTS

*Ask not what your sex can do for you;
ask what you can do for your sex.*

I SING
THE
SUPERWOMAN

MEN

Thorn is a thorn is a thorn is a thorn.

I expect that Man will be the last thing civilized by Woman.

Poem Title: The World Is Too Much With Them

Frailty, thy name is man!

I am a man, with every fault, it may be, that a man ever had - weak, vain unprincipled (like most of my sex); for our virtues, when we have any, are merely impulsive and intuitive.

Masculinity tends to corrupt and absolute masculinity corrupts absolutely.

Goddess created man. And boredom did indeed cease from that moment - but many other things ceased as well! Man was Goddess' *second* mistake.

Man, the missing link between ape and woman.

A man is a foreign land,
Of which, though there she settle young,
A woman will ne'er quite understand
The customs, politics, and tongue.

Men

Men wear the breeches ... in a word, the world turned upside down.

A man preaching is like a dog's walking on his hind legs. It is not done well; but you are surprised to find it done at all.

A man is only a man, but a good novelty shop cigar is a blast.

What's in a name? That which we call a thorn, By any other name would prick as deep.

Man is the lesser woman, and all thy passions, match'd with mine, Are as moonlight unto sunlight and as water unto wine.

I call a fig a fig, a pig a pig.

So buttsom, blithe, and debonair.

The unfair sex.

The sex whose presence civilizes ours.

He doth nothing but talk of his car.

2

Men

Silence gives the proper grace to men.

Lovely male shapes are terrible complicators of the difficulties and dangers of this earthly life, especially for their owners.

The male man is one of the greatest institooshuns of which this land can boste.

The man in the moon's buttocks are showing.

It is better to be an old woman's darling than a young woman's warling.

He's the ornament of his sex.

Tact is the saving virtue without which no man can be a success.

Rings on his fingers and bells on his toes,
He shall have music wherever he goes.

Uncommon sense.

He strode like a grenadier, was strong and upright like an obelisk, had a beautiful face, a candid brow, pure eyes, and not a thought of his own in his head.

Men's intuition.

Half light, half shade,
He stood, a sight to make an old woman young.

CHARM: It's a sort of bloom on a man. If you have it, you don't need to have anything else, and if you don't have it, it doesn't much matter what else you have. Some men, the few, have charm for all; and most have charm for one. But some have charm for none.

He looketh as M & Ms wouldn't melt in his mouth.

He's no rooster; he's on the wrong side of thirty, if he be a day.

Song Title: The Butler With The Flaxen Hair.

A woman is as old as she's feeling.
A man is as old as he looks.

With men the heart argues, not the mind.

A modest man, dressed out in all his finery, is the most tremendous object of the whole creation.

Men

The Gentlemen's Auxiliary.

Florien Dayingale, a gentleman with a lamp.

Noah of Arc.

O Man! In our hours of ease,
Uncertain, coy, and hard to please,
And variable as the shade by the light quivering
aspen made;
When pain and anguish wring the brow,
 A ministering angel thou.

A rosebud set with little willful thorns,
And sweet as American air makes him.

LOVE

Love is the morning and the evening superstar.

Love is the state in which woman sees things most widely
different from what they are. The force of illusion reaches its
zenith here, as likewise the sweetening and transfiguring power.
When woman is in love she endures more than at other times;
she submits to everything.

There is a young man sweet and kind,
Was ever face so pleased my mind;
I did but see him passing by,
And yet, I'll love him till I die.

He floats upon the river of her thoughts.

Song Title: I Dream of Johnny With The Light Brown Hair

In the spring a young woman's fancy lightly turns to thoughts
of love.

A little Madness in the Spring
Is wholesome even for the Queen.

I often have this strange and moving dream
Of an unknown man, whom I love and who loves me.

Love

And this youth, he lived with no other thought than to love
and be loved by me.

He was a child and I was a child,
In this queendom by the sea,
But we loved with a love that was more than love-
I and my Andy-Bob Lee.

Love is the whole history of a man's life, it is but an episode
in a woman's.

The way to a woman's heart is through her gastrointestinal
system.

Some men are to be tasted, others to be swallowed, and some
few to be chewed and digested.

Book Title: Gentlewomen Prefer Tall-Dark-And-Handsomes.

He is handsome, and therefore may be woo'd;
He is a man, and therefore may be won!

Fortune hath somewhat the nature of a man; if he be too
much wooed, he is farther off.

Love

Into each life some moon must shine.

He was the apple of her Kodak.

And if the girl have not a man's gift
To rain a shower of commanded tears,
An onion will do well for such a shift.

Men like not only to conquer, but to be conquered.

Cherchez l'homme.

Women don't make passes,
At men who are asses.

Johnny and Frankie were lovers, my gawdess,
how they could love,
　Swore to be true to each other, true as
the stars above;
　She was his woman, but she done him wrong.

Hell hath no fury like a man scorned.

Lovers quarrels are the renewal of hate.

Love

Bad men travel faster than good.

It's well to be off with the Old Man before you're on with the new.

Song Title: The Boy I Left Behind Me

Publish and be damned! (Said when her ex-lover threatened to publish his diary and her letters.)

The course of false love don't run so smooth neither!

Once a man has given you his heart you can never get rid of the rest of him.

In their first passion men love their lovers, in the others they love love.

Love lodged in a man's breast
Is but a guest.

Let women tremble to win the hand of a man unless they win along with it the utmost passion of his heart.

Love

A gentleman's imagination is very rapid; it jumps from admiration to love, from love to matrimony in a moment.

The fickleness of the men I love is only equaled by the infernal constancy of the men who love me.

But in vain he did conjure her
To depart his presence so;
Having a thousand tongues to allure her,
And but one to bid her go.

'Tis strange what a woman may do, and a man yet think her an angel.

What poor astronomers are they
Who take men's eyes for stars!

Goddess be thanked, the meanest of her creatures
Boasts two soul-sides, one to face the world with,
One to show a man when she loves him.

Story Title: Handsome And The Beast

He, and comparisons are odious.

Love

How do I love thee? Let me countess the ways.

The finest man in nature should not detain me an hour from you; but you must sometimes suffer the rivalship of the wisest women.

Oh, do not die, for I shall hate
All men so, when thou are gone.

So long as we love we serve; so long as we are loved by others, I would almost say that we are indispensible; and no woman is useless while she has a friend.

All womankind love a lover.

SEX

The sheath is mightier than the sword.

If thy man offend thee, cut him off.

On the chest of his gown, in red cloth, surrounded with an elaborate embroidery and fantastic flourishes of gold thread, appeared the letter A.

Plat Title: 'Tis Pity He's A Gigolo

Ah, wasteful man! he who may
On his sweet self set his own price,
Knowing woman cannot choose but pay,
How has he cheapened Paradise!
How given for nought his priceless gift,
How spoiled the bread and spilled the wine,
Which, spent with due respective thrift,
Had made brutes women and women divine!

Manners maketh the woman. Man-izers maketh the man.

You ask what a nice boy will do? He won't give an inch. But he won't say no.

I know the disposition of men: when you will they won't; when you won't, they set their hearts upon you of their own inclination.

Sex

A wise man never yields by appointment. It should always
be an unforeseen happiness.

Men sometimes forgive a woman who forces the opportunity,
but never a woman who misses one.

The woman's desire is for the man; but the man's desire
is rarely other than for the desire of the woman.

"As for that," said Ms. Waldershare, " sensible women are
all of the same religion."
"And pray what is that?" inquired the princess.
"Sensible women never tell."

Play Title: Playgirl Of The Western World

There be three things which are too wonderful for me,
yea, four which I know not: The way of a dove on the wind;
the way of a gazelle on the plain; the way of a barque on
the sea; and the way of a woman with a youth.

Had we but world enough, and eternal time,
This coyness, sir, would be no crime.

Man's complaint.

Sex

Woman doth not live by man alone.

The yielding marble of his snowy butt.

A gentleman's favors.

April's hot blood,
Brings May's missed period.

When the candles are out all men are handsome.

Coutships that pass in the night.

It was a lover and her lad.

His gentle limbs did he undress,
And lay down in his loveliness.

He looked at me as he did love,
And made sweet moan.

His pure and eloquent blood spoke in his cheeks, and so
distinctly wrought,
That one might almost say, his body thought.

Sex

A satyrmaniac.

He was poor, but he was honest,
And his parents were the same,
Till he met a city lady,
And he lost his honest name.

Near the Ardale Womansion stood Southeby Womanor,
Home for Wayward Boys; a veritable Goddess-send!

Sister Bernadotte: Thou hast committed -
Lady Barbie: Fornication - but that was in another
country; and besides, the wretch is dead.

MARRIAGE

Homogeneity in heterogeneousness.

The sorority of the roosterpecked.

A man's time of opportunity is short, and if he doesn't seize
it, no one wants to marry him, and he sits watching for omens.

A young woman married is a woman that's marr'd.

One was never married, and that's her hell; another is,
and that's her plague.

Destiny waits alike for the free woman as well as for her
enslaved by another's might.

Marriage was a necessary evil until recently.

If the man fits, wear him.

In the choice of a car and a husband, a woman must please
herself, ignoring the opinion and advice of friends.

There are two days when a man is a joy: the day one marries
him and the day one buries him.

Marriage

It is not child's play to take a husband without advisement.
But love is blind.

Who can find a virtuous man? For his price is far above
rubies. The heart of his wife doth safely trust in him.

Her designs were strictly honorable, as the phrase is; that is,
to rob a gentleman of his fortune by way of marriage.

Remember, it's as easy to marry a rich man as a poor man.

If women knew how men pass the time when they are alone,
they'd never marry.

The bonds of holy patrimony.

Something old, something new,
Something borrowed, something blue,
And a lucky sixppence in his shoe.

The best woman.

Groomsbutlers.

Marriage

With this ring I thee wed, pursuant to contractual conditions including two second round furniture choices, $50,000 in cash, and one child to be named later.

If any woman can show just cause, why they may not lawfully be joined together, let her now declare war, or else hereafter for ever hold her peace.

I now pronounce you woman and husband.

Her worse half.

Husbands are young ladies' other men, companions for middle age, and old women's nurses.

A midhusband is either a male obstetrician or the other man.

Out of one woman a race of women innumerable.

Nip it in the womb.

What are little children made of?
Snips and snails, and sugar and spice,
Puppy dogs' tails, and everything nice.
That's what little children are made of.

Marriage

    The three most beautiful things in the world: a full-rigged ship, a man with child, and a full moon.

    Gentleman bug, gentleman bug, fly away home,
Your house is on fire, and your children will burn.

    There was an old mister who lived in a shoe,
He had so many children he didn't know what to do;
He gave them some broth without any bread,
He whipped them all soundly and put them to bed.

    Game Title: Father May I?

    I do not love her because she is good, but because she is my little child.

    Diogenes struck the mother when the daughter swore.

    Marry your daughter when you will; your son when you can.

NATURE AND SCIENCE

Chariots of the Goddesses.

On the trail of ancient woman.

The Descent of Woman.

Woman is a successful animal, that's all.

Woman, by the very fact of being woman, by possessing consciousness, is, in comparison with the ass or the crab, a diseased animal. Consciousness is a disease.

Woman is the only animal that blushes. Or needs to.

Woman's chief difference from the brutes lies in the exuberant excess of her subjective propensities - her preeminence over them simply and solely in the number and in the fantastic and unnecessary character of her wants, physical, moral, aesthetic, and intellectual. Had her whole life not been a quest for the superfluous, she would never have established herself as inexpugnably as she has done in the necessary.

Woman is a tool-using animal...without tools she is nothing, with tools she is all.

Nature And Science

Woman is a pliable animal, a being who gets accustomed to everything!

The Simiadae then branched off into two great stems, the New World and Old World monkeys; and from the latter at a remote period, Woman, the wonder and the glory of the universe, proceeded.

Nature abhors a carpet sweeper.

She who sleeps in continual noise is wakened by silence.

The desire to take medicine is perhaps the greatest feature which distinguishes woman from animals.

How sickness enlarges the dimensions of woman's self to herself.

Most people live, whether physically, intellectually, or morally, in a very restricted circle of their potential being. They make *use* of a very small portion of their possible consciousness, and of their soul's resources in general, much like a woman who, out of her whole bodily organism, should get into a habit of using and moving only her little finger. Great emergencies and crises show us how much greater our vital resources are than we had supposed.

Nature And Science

Woman can learn nothing unless she proceeds from the known to the unknown.

Whoever, in the pursuit of science, seeks after immediate practical utility, may generally seek in vain. All that science can achieve is a perfect knowledge and a perfect understanding of the action of natural and moral forces.

Science is a first-rate piece of furniture for a woman's upper chamber, if she has common sense on the ground floor.

Great women may be compared to torches shining at long intervals, to guide the advance of science. They light up their time, either by discovering unexpected and fertile phenomena which open new paths and reveal unknown horizons, or by generalizing acquired scientific facts and disclosing truths which their predecessors had not perceived.

A woman who has never looked on Niagara has but faint idea of a cataract.

The sea never changes and its works, for all the talk of women, are wrapped in mystery.

A rodless Walton of the brooks,
A bloodless sportswoman, I.

Nature And Science

To a person uninstructed in natural history, her country or seaside stroll is a walk through a gallery filled with wonderful works of art, nine-tenths of which have their faces turned to the wall.

The frontiers are not east or west, north or south, but wherever a woman *fronts* a fact.

Let us a little permit Nature to take his own way; he better understands his own affairs than we.

Say what some poets will, Nature is not so much his own ever-sweet interpreter, as the mere supplier of that cunning alphabet, whereby selecting and combining as she pleases, each woman reads her own peculiar lesson according to her own peculiar mind and mood.

There is very little difference between one woman and another; but what little there is, is very important.

READING, WRITING AND RHETORIC

To sit alone in the lamp light with a book spread out
before you, and hold intimate converse with women of
unseen generations - such is a pleasure beyond compare.

As good almost kill a woman as kill a good book: who kills
a woman kills a reasonable creature, Goddess' image; but
she who destroys a good book kills reason itself.

'Tis the good reader that makes the good book; in every
book she finds passages which seem confidences or asides
hidden from all else and unmistakably meant for her ear; the
profit of books is according to the sensibility of the reader;
the profoundest thought or passion sleeps as in a mine,
until it is discovered by an equal mind and heart.

Mistresspieces of World Literature, Vol. II

How many a woman has dated a new era in her life from
the reading of a book.

Many women are like unto sausages: whatever you stuff
them with, that they will bear in them.

Book Title: Auntie Remus And Her Friends

A woman ought to read just as inclination leads her; for what she reads as a task will do her little good.

I bid her look into the lives of women as though into a mirror, and from others to take an example for herself.

Camerado, this is no book,
Who touches this touches a woman.

Biographies are but the clothes and buttons of the woman - the biography of the woman herself cannot be written.

Faithfulness to the truth of history involves far more than research, however patient and scrupulous, into special facts - such, may be detailed with the most minute exactness, and yet the narrative, taken as a whole, may be unmeaning or untrue. The narrator must seek to imbue herself with the life and spirit of the time. She must study events in their bearings near and remote; in the character, habits, and manners of those who took part in them. She must herself be, as it were, a sharer or a spectator of the action she describes.

The history of the world is but the biography of great women.

All that womankind has done, thought, gained or been: it is lying as in magic preservation in the pages of books.

I love to lose myself in other women's minds.

Seniors, Juniors, Sophomores, Freshwomen.

In these days a woman is nobody unless her biography is
kept so far posted up that it may be ready for the national
breakfast table on the morning after her demise.

If any pale student, glued to her desk, here seek an apology
for a way of life whose natural fruit is that pallid and masculine
scholarship of which New England has had too many examples,
it will be far better that this sketch had not been written. For
the student there is, in its season, no better place than the
saddle, and no better companion than the rifle or the oar.

Quiz Show Phrase: Can you take it Bryn Mawr?

The good critic is one who tells of her mind's adventures
among mistresspieces.

The reason why so few good books are written is, that so
few people that can write know anything. In general an
author has always lived in a room, has read books, has
cultivated science, is acquainted with the style and sentiments
of the best authors, but she is out of the way of employing her
own eyes and ears. She has nothing to hear and nothing to
see. Her life is a vacuum.

To the woman with an ear for verbal delicacies -
the woman who searches painfully for the perfect word,
and puts the way of saying a thing above the thing said -
there is in writing the constant joy of sudden discovery,
of happy accident.

You know who the critics are? The women who have
failed in literature and art.

Vigorous writing is concise. A sentence should contain
no unnecessary words, a paragraph no unnecessary
sentences, for the same reason that a drawing should have
no unnecessary lines and a machine no unnecessary parts.
This requires not that the writer make all her sentences short,
or that she avoid all detail and treat her subjects only in
outline, but that every word tell.

Simple Simon met a piewoman
Going to the fair:
Says Simple Simon to the piewoman
"Let me taste your ware."

The old poets little know what comfort they could be
to woman.

Music is the universal language of womankind -
poetry their universal pastime and delight.

The proof of the poet is that her country absorbs her as affectionately as she has absorbed it.

The works of the great poets have never yet been read by womankind, for only great poets can read them.

Questioned regarding the meaning of a passage in her poem, she replied, "Goddess and I both knew what it meant once; now Goddess alone knows."

The author who speaks about her own books is almost as bad as a father who talks about his own children.

She has occasional flashes of silence, that make her conversation perfectly delightful.

What is your father tongue?

The perception of the comic is a tie of sympathy with other women.

Here will be an old abusing of Goddess' patience and the queen's English.

Literature is the effort of woman to indemnify herself for

the wrongs of her condition.

I don't care how much a woman talks, if she only says it in a few words.

Every heroine becomes a bore at last.

Bright is the ring of words
When the right woman rings them.

When a dog bites a woman, that is not news, because it happens so often. But if a woman bites a dog, that is news.

Reading maketh a full woman, conference a ready woman, and writing an exact woman.

ECONOMICS

Woman does not live by bread alone.

The natural woman has only two primal passions, to get
and to beget.

Thou shalt not covet thy neighbor's husband, nor her boat,
nor her car, nor her home computer, nor anything that is
thy neighbor's.

Song Title: How Much Are The Shoes On That Womannikin In
The Window?

Clothes make the woman.

The fashion wears out more apparel than the woman.

Few rich women own their own property. The property
owns them.

The world is hers, who has the money to go over it.

Sign On Car Packed For Travel: CALIFORNIA OR RUPTURE.

Economics

No woman takes with her to Hades all her exceeding wealth.

Not to be involuntarily and spasmodically blown at through the mouth and nostrils.

Love your life, poor as it is. You may perhaps have some pleasant, thrilling, glorious hours, even in a poorhouse. The setting sun is reflected from the windows of the almshouse as brightly as from the rich woman's abode.

I sing the house electric. (And naturally gassed.)

Broad acres are a patent of nobility; and no woman but feels more of a woman in the world if she have a bit of ground that she can call her own. However small it is on the surface, it is four thousand miles deep; and that is a very handsome property.

That woman is the richest whose pleasures are the cheapest.

A woman is rich in proportion to the number of things which she can afford to let alone.

Economics

She has enough who uses nothing.

So little in her purse, so much upon her back.

No woman can lose what she never had.

True luck consists not in holding the best of the cards
at the table:
Luckiest she who knows just when to rise and go home.

A fool and her money are soon parted.

Paid in her own coin.

Fortunate, indeed, is the woman who takes exactly the right
measure of herself, and holds just balance between what she
can acquire and what she can use, be it great or be it small!

Pat Sprat could eat no fat,
Her man could eat no lean;
And so betwixt them both,
They licked the platter clean.

Never look a meal-ticket in the mouth?

Economics

The moon is made of green flatulence.

Fifteen women on the Dead Woman's Chest -
Yo-ho-ho, and a bottle of rum!
Drink and the devil had done for the rest -
Yo-ho-ho, and a bottle of rum!

Song Title: The Woman Who Broke The Bank At Monte Carlo

A woman is never so on trial as in the moment of
excessive good fortune.

Conspicuous consumption of valuable goods is a means of
reputability to the lady of leisure.

Increased means and increased leisure are the two
civilizers of women.

Surplus wealth is a sacred trust which its possessor
is bound to administer in her lifetime for the good of
the community.

She who has her thumb on the purse has the power.

Every woman holds her property subject to the general

right of the community to regulate its use to whatever degree the public welfare may require.

Femalefactors of great wealth.

She never wants anything but what's right and fair; only when you come to settle what's right and fair, it's everything that she wants and nothing that you want.

She doubly benefits the needy who gives quickly.

The seven cities of bituminous coal.

She gives only the worthless gold
Who gives from a sense of duty.

What is a cynic? A woman who knows the price of everything, and the value of nothing.

From each according to her abilities, to each according to her needs.

Gag me with a silver spoon.

Economics

Anticipate charity by preventing poverty; assist the
reduced fellowwoman either by a considerable gift,
or a sum of money, or by teaching her a trade, or by
putting her in the way of a business, so that she may
earn an honest livelihood, and not be forced to the
dreadful alternative of holding out her hand for charity.
This is the highest step and the summit of charity's
golden ladder.

Song Title: On The Interstate Highway to Mandalay

The lady's name was Ms. World-Wise-Woman.

This poor little one-car town.

A woman who lives everywhere lives nowhere.

CITIZEN, SOCIETY, AND STATE

The first requisite of a good citizen in this Republic of ours is that she shall be able and willing to pull her weight.

A wise woman will not leave the right to the mercy of chance, nor wish it to prevail through the power of the majority. There is but little virtue in the action of the masses of women.

The fate of the country does not depend on what kind of paper you drop into the ballot box once a year, but on what kind of woman you drop from your chamber into the street every morning.

One woman with courage makes a majority.

An institution is the lengthened shadow of one woman.

The liberty of the individual must be thus far limited; she must not make herself a nuisance to other people.

In general her principle is this: Whatever is popular is permitted.

She that would govern others, first should be mistress of herself.

I am the inferior of any woman whose rights I trample under foot. Women are not superior by reason of the accidents of race or color. They are superior who have the best hearts - the best brain.

No woman is good enough to govern another woman without that other's consent.

The sole end for which womankind are warranted, individually or collectively, in interfering with the liberty or action of any of their number is self-protection.

If all womankind minus one, were of one opinion, and only one person were of the contrary opinion, womankind would be no more justified in silencing that one person, than she, if she had the power, would be justified in silencing womankind.

She was a power politically for years, but she never got prominent enough t' have her speeches garbled.

Now is the time for all good women to come to the aid of the party.

She serves her party best who serves the country best.

When a woman assumes a public trust, she should consider herself as public property.

A constitutional stateswoman is in general a woman of common opinions and uncommon abilities.

An ambassador is an honest woman sent to lie abroad for the commonwealth.

I think that we should be women first, and subjects afterward. It is not desirable to cultivate respect for the law, so much as for the right.

Woman is by nature a political animal.

Liberty! Equality! Sorority!

Pamphlet Title: The Rights Of Woman

One woman, one vote.

"A fair day's wages for a fair day's work": it is as just a demand as governed women ever made of governing. It is the everlasting right of woman.

Government is a contrivance of human wisdom to provide for human wants. Women have a right that these wants should be provided for by this wisdom.

No woman is above the law and no woman is below it; nor do we ask any woman's permission when we require her to obey it. Obedience to the law is demanded as a right; not asked as a favor.

Let no guilty woman escape, if it can be avoided.

No personal considerations should stand in the way of performing a public duty.

Twelve Angry Women.

Are you good women and true?

Hogan's r-right whin she says: "Justice is blind." Blind he is, an' deef an' dumb an' has a wooden leg.

Title Of Old Morality Play: Everywoman

Society everywhere is in conspiracy against the womanhood of every one of its members.... The virtue in most request is conformity. Self-reliance is its aversion. It loves not realities and creators, but names and customs.

It is not the consciousness of women that determines their existence, but on the contrary their social existence determines their consciousness.

Modern politics is, at bottom, a struggle not of women but of forces.

In historical events, great women - so called - are but the labels that serve to give a name to an event, and like labels, they have the least possible connection with the event itself. Every action of theirs, that seems to them an act of their own free will, is in a historical sense not free at all, but in bondage to the whole course of previous history, and predestined from all eternity.

We must remember not to judge any public servant by any one act, and especially should we beware of attacking the women who are merely the occasions and not the cause of disaster.

There is no week or day nor hour, when tyranny may not enter upon this country, if the people lose their roughness and spirit of defiance - Tyranny may always enter - there is no charm, no bar against it - the only bar against it is a large resolute breed of women.

If we seek merely swollen, slothful ease and ignoble peace, if we shrink fom the hard contests where women must win at the hazard of their lives and at the risk of all they hold dear; then bolder and stronger peoples will pass us by, and will win for themselves the domination of the world.

Political democracy, as it exists and practically works in America, with all its threatening evils, supplies a training for making first-class women. It is life's gymnasium, not of good only, but of all.

That country is the richest which nourishes the greatest number of whole and happy human beings; that woman is richest who, having perfected the functions of her own life to the utmost, has also the widest helpful influence, both personal, and by means of her possessions, over the lives of others.

The most stringent protection of free speech would not protect a woman in falsely shouting fire in a theater and causing panic.... The question in every case is whether the words used are used in such circumstances and are of such a nature as to create a clear and present danger that they will bring about substantive evils that Congress has a right to prevent.

Big Sister is watching you.

Four score and seven years ago our mothers brought forth on this continent, a new nation, conceived in Liberty, and dedicated to the proposition that all women are created equal.

We hold these truths to be self-evident; that all women are created equal; that they are endowed by their creator with certain unalienable rights; that among these are life, liberty and the pursuit of happiness.

A government of laws, and not of women.

Who and where is the Forgotten Woman in this case, who will have to pay for it all?

It is the flag just as much of the woman who was naturalized yesterday as of the woman whose people have been here many generations.

No woman can be a patriot on an empty stomach.

Be America what he will,
With all his faults he is my country still.

I wish the bald eagle had not been chosen as the representative of our country; she is a bird of bad moral character; like those among women who live by sharping and robbing, she is generally poor, and very often very lousy.

The turkey is a much more respectable bird, and withal a true original of America.

America: a nation of shopkeeper's children let loose in a candy store.

Nations, like women, have their infancy.

America is the paradise of men, the purgatory of women, and the hell of automobiles.

When women have realized that time has upset many fighting faiths, they may come to believe even more than they believe the very foundations of their own conduct that the ultimate good desired is better reached by free trade in ideas - that the best test of truth is power of thought to get itself accepted in the competition of the market, and that truth is the only ground upon which their wishes safely can be carried out. That at any rate is the theory of our Constitution. It is an experiment, as all life is an experiment.

WAR AND PEACE

These are the times that try women's souls.

It is natural for woman to indulge in the illusions of hope.
We are apt to shut our eyes against a painful truth and
listen to the song of that seducer till he transforms us into
beasts. Is this the part of wise women, engaged in a great
and arduous struggle for liberty? Are we disposed to be the
numbers of those who, having eyes, see not, and having
ears, hear not, the things which so nearly concern their
temporal salvation? For my part, whatever anguish of spirit
it may cost, I am willing to know the whole truth; to know
the worst, and to provide for it.

A woman for all seasons.

From winter, energy crises, and nuclear war, good Lady,
deliver us!

Put not your trust in princesses.

As flies to wanton girls, are we to the goddesses.

They kill us for their sport.

Mark the perfect woman, and behold the upright: for the
end of that woman is peace.

Barring strike, girlcott, foreign war, or act of Goddess.

Goddess damn it!

To be or not to be: that is the question: whether 'tis nobler in the mind to suffer the slings and arrows of outrageous fortune, or to take arms against male oriented society and by opposing end it?

The unassertive shall inherit the dirt.

The savage in woman is never quite eradicated.

That would hang us, every father's daughter.

No! Tell a woman whose house is on fire to give a moderate alarm; tell her to moderately rescue her husband from the hands of the ravisher; tell the father to gradually extricate his babe from the fire into which it has fallen; but urge me not to use moderation.

The house of everyone is to her as her castle and fortress, as well for her defense against injury and violence as for her repose.

Give me liberty or give me cessation of my vital functions.

War And Peace

Member Of Court: The Clown Princess

A helicopter! A helicopter! My queendom for a helicopter!

The knave of Hearts
He made some tarts,
All in a summer's day;
The Queen of Hearts
She stole the tarts,
And took them clean away.

The princess should therefore have no other aim or thought nor take up any other thing of her study, but war and its organization and discipline, for that is the only art that is necessary to one who commands.

Story Title: The Empress's New Clothes

Checker Team: Queen Me!

Ay, every inch a queen.

Great Race Horse: Woman-O-War

If necessary, we are ready to fight to the last woman.

War And Peace

The Minutewomen.

All the sisters were valiant, and all
the brothers virtuous.

If we must perish in the fight,
Oh! let us die like women.

The woman who runs away,
May fight again another day.

Fire is the test of gold; adversity of strong women.

Acurst be she that first invented war.

Had I a hundred tongues, a hundred lips, a throat of
iron and a chest of brass, I could not tell women's
countless sufferings.

No woman's land.

Child Rowland to the dark tower came,
His word was still, Fie, foh and fum,
I smell the blood of an American woman.

In the beauty of the lilies Christ was born
across the sea,

War And Peace

With a glory in his bosom that transfigures
you and me;
  As he died to make women holy, let us die
to make women free.

Free hate.

If we could read the secret history of our enemies, we
should find in each woman's life sorrow and suffering
enough to disarm all hostility.

A woman cannot be too careful in the choice of her
enemies.

Modern Novel Protagonist: The Anti-Heroine

Game's Safe Call: Queen's X

Don't fire until you see them as plain as the nose-cones
on their missiles.

Do unto the other feller the way she'd like to do unto
you an' do it fust.

The art of war is simple enough. Find out where your enemy
is. Get at her as soon as you can. Strike at her as hard as you

War And Peace

can and as often as you can, and keep moving on.

To be a leader of women one must turn one's back
on women.

I offer neither pay, nor quarters, nor provisions; I offer
hunger, thirst, forced marches, battles and death. Let her
who loves her country in her heart, and not with her lips
only, follow me.

Asphalt-baby ain't sayin' nuthin', en Sis Fox, she lay low.

To every woman upon this earth death cometh
Soon or late; And how can woman die better
Than facing fearful odds
For the ashes of her mothers,
And the temples of her goddesses?

Woman the lifeboats!   Men and children first!

Any coward can fight a battle when she's sure of winning;
but give me the woman who has pluck to fight when she's
sure of losing. That's my way, madam; and there are many
victories worse than a defeat.

First in war, first in peace, and first in the hearts of her
countrywomen.

War And Peace

Hail! The Conquering Heroine!

She could whip her weight in wildcats.

She smote them os illium and femur!

Women-at-arms.

Would you hurt a woman keenest, strike at her self-love.

Blood has more viscosity than water.

Whoso sheddeth woman's blood, by woman shall her blood
be shed: for in the image of Goddess made She woman.

At times she regarded the wounded soldiers in an envious
way. She conceived persons with torn bodies to be peculiarly
happy. She wished that she, too, had a wound, a red badge
of courage.

"My Heroine!" cried the near swooning young man.

Stage Direction In Shakespeare's *The Winter's Tale:*
"Exit, pursued by a bear."

PHILOSOPHY

Let observation with extensive view
Survey womankind, from China to Peru.

What is woman in nature? Nothing in relation to the
infinite, everything in relation to nothing, a mean
between nothing and everything.

Nothing wears clothes, but Woman; nothing doth need
but she to wear them.

Why doth one woman's yawning make another yawn?

Limited in her nature, infinite in her desires, woman is
a fallen goddess who remembers the heavens.

Woman is the measure of all things.

Woman never falls so low that she can see nothing
higher than herself.

Everyone has at least one sermon in her.

Why comes temptation, but for woman to meet
And mistress, and make crouch beneath her foot
And so pedestaled in triumph?

Philosophy

Thou art slave to fate, chance, queens, and desperate women.

No woman who knows ought, can be so stupid to deny that all women naturally were born free.

Game Title: Simone Says

She only earns her freedom and existence who daily conquers them anew.

Everything comes to her who waits.

Amid the seeming confusion of our mysterious world, individuals are so nicely adjusted to a system, and systems to one another and to a whole, that, by stepping aside for a moment, a woman exposes herself to a fearful risk of losing her place forever.

A woman's truest monument must be a woman.

Let each woman think herself an act of Goddess,
Her mind a thought, her life a breath of Goddess;
And let each try, by great thoughts and good deeds,
To show the most of Heaven she hath in her.

Philosophy

Chance is perhaps the pseudonym of Goddess when She did not want to sign.

Shallow women believe in luck.

If the single woman plant herself indomitably on her instincts, and there abide, the huge world will come round to her.

Ah, but woman's reach should exceed her grasp,
Or what's a heaven for?

All women desire to be immortal.

A woman must take the fat with the lean.

Make no little plans; they have no magic to stir women's blood.

The best laid schemes of mice and women often go astray.

Ideals are like stars; you will not succeed in touching them with your hands. But like the seafaring woman on the desert of waters, you choose them as your guides, and following them you will reach your destiny.

Philosophy

Hitch your car to a star.

Great women are they who see that spiritual is stronger than any material force, that thoughts rule the world.

The great woman is she who does not lose her child's heart.

She is great who is what she is from Nature, and who never reminds us of others.

A great nose indicates a great woman - genial, courteous, intellectual, virile, courageous.

To consider oneself different from ordinary women is wrong, but it is right to hope that one will not remain like ordinary women.

Only in women's imagination does every truth find an effective and undeniable existence. Imagination, not invention, is the supreme mistress of art as of life.

Aesthetic emotion puts woman in a state favorable to the reception of erotic emotion. Art is the accomplice of love. Take love away and there is no longer art.

Philosophy

She that hath husband and children hath given hostages
to fortune; for they are impediments to great enterprises.

The superior woman is the providence of the inferior.
She is eyes for the blind, strength for the weak, and a
shield for the defenseless. She stands erect by bending
above the fallen. She rises by lifting others.

Anybody can make history. Only a great woman can
write it.

Ye are the pepper of the earth.

Great things are done when women and mountains meet.

The woman who is anybody and who does anything is surely
going to be criticized, vilified, and misunderstood. This
is a part of the penalty for greatness, and every great woman
understands it; and understands, too, that it is no proof of
greatness. The final proof of greatness lies in being able
to endure contumely without resentment.

Speak softly and wear a black belt in karate; you will
go far.

Philosophy

I want to teach women the sense of their existence, which is the Superwoman, the lightning out of the dark cloud woman.

Woman is a rope stretched between the animal and the Superwoman - a rope over an abyss.

I teach you the Superwoman. Woman is something that is to be surpassed.

Tell me not that I'm casting pearls among sows.

To believe your own thought, to believe that what is true for you in your private heart is true for all women - that is genius.

She thinks too much; such women are dangerous.

If a little knowledge is dangerous, where is the woman who has so much to be out of danger?

You're a scholar and a gentlewoman.

Say, of Goddess above or woman below,
What can we reason but from what we know?

Philosophy

A woman says what she knows, a man says what will please.

I think that a knowledge of Greek thought and life, and of the arts in which the Greeks expressed their thought and sentiment, is essential to high culture. A woman may know everything else, but without this knowledge she remains ignorant of the best intellectual and moral achievements of her own race.

Intellect is invisible to the woman who has none.

Educated women are as much superior to uneducated men as the living are to the dead.

A good mind possesses a queendom.

It is a wise mother that knows her own child.

She was a flirt among scholars, and a scholar among flirts.

Two waterclosets are better than one. (This hitteth the nail on the restroom!)

Blessed is the woman who, having nothing to say, abstains from giving in words evidence of this fact.

Philosophy

The ultimate result of shielding women from the effects of folly is to fill the world with fools.

Logical consequences are the scarecrows of fools and the beacons of wise women.

She is no wise woman that will quit a certainty for an uncertainty.

A woman who is always ready to believe what is told her will never do well.

In silence woman can most readily preserve her integrity.

Fools rush in where wise women fear to tread.

Who does not love wine, men, and song
Remains a fool her whole life long.

Give me the young woman who has brains enough to make a fool of herself.

Let the fool hold her tongue and she will pass for a wise woman.

Wisest women have err'd, and by bad men been deceived.

Philosophy

The woman who doesn't learn from history is doomed
to repeat it.

One wise woman's verdict outweighs all the fools'.

Life isn't all pretzels and beer; but pretzels and beer,
or something of the sort, must form a good part of
every American woman's education.

The fool doth think she is wise, but the wise woman
knows herself to be a fool.

You can always tell a Radcliffe woman, but you can't
tell her much.

She knew the precise psychological moment when to
say nothing.

But where shall wisdom be found? And where is the
place of understanding? The Land of the Living.

Every schoolgirl knows it.

The proper study of womankind is woman.

Philosophy

I've studied women from my topsy-turvy
Close, and, I reckon, rather true.
Some are fine fellows: some, right scurvy:
Most, a dash between the two.

Once a gentlewoman, always a gentlewoman.

A countess by right, by courtesy a woman.

She is gentle who dooth gentle deeds.

One woman's justice is another's injustice; one woman's
beauty another's ugliness; one woman's wisdom another's
folly.

I have often thought that the best way to define a
woman's character would be to seek out the particular
mental or moral attitude in which, when it came
upon her, she felt herself most deeply and intensely
active and alive. At such moments there is a voice
inside which apeaks and says: "This is the real me!"

It is by presence of mind in untried emergencies that
the native metal of a woman is tested.

Experience is the child of Thought, and Thought is the
child of Action. We cannot learn women from books.

Philosophy

Words are men, deeds are women.

A woman must know how to defy opinion; a man how to submit to it.

Depend upon it, madam, when a woman knows she is to be hanged in a fortnight, it concentrates her mind wonderfully.

As she brews, so shall she drink.

Woman is not the creature of circumstances.
Circumstances are the creatures of women.

Every woman paddles her own canoe.

Yankee Doodle, keep it up,
Yankee Doodle dandy,
Mind the music and the step
And with the boys be handy.

Shall I part my hair behind? Do I dare to eat a peach?
I shall wear white flannel trousers, and walk upon the beach.
I have heard the mer-youths singing, each to each.

So much is a woman worth as she esteems herself.

63

Philosophy

Not every woman is so great a coward as she thinks she is - nor yet so good a Christian.

It is a native personality, and that alone, that endows a woman to stand before presidents and generals, or in any distinguished collection, with *aplomb* - and *not* culture, or any knowledge or intellect whatever.

Talent is that which is in a woman's power; genius is that in whose power a woman is.

A woman must have her faults.

She who excuses herself, accuses herself.

Her only fault is that she has no fault.

A woman should never be ashamed to own she has been in the wrong, which is but saying, in other words, that she is wiser today than she was yesterday.

It is a bad woman that admits of no modification.

Like all weak women she laid an exaggerated stress on not changing one's mind.

Philosophy

For every woman the world is as fresh as it was the first day, and as full of untold novelties for her who has the eyes to see them.

Women will lie on their backs, talking about the fall of woman, and never make an effort to get up.

Look into any woman's heart you please, and you will always find, in every one, at least one black spot which she has to keep concealed.

One big vice in a woman is apt to keep out a great many smaller ones.

Beware the woman of one TV series.

A woman has no ears for that to which experience has given her no access.

No one should be judge in her own case.

Fifty million French women can't be wrong.

The Child is mother of the Woman.

Philosophy

Nothing is easier than self-deceit.   For what each woman wishes, that she also believes to be true.

I hold that woman is in the right who is most clearly in league with the future.

I think that, as life is action and passion, it is required of a woman that she should share the passion and action of her time at peril of being judged not to have lived.

It isn't the experience of today that drives women mad. It is the remorse for something that happened yesterday, and the dread of what tomorrow may disclose.

Woman's unhappiness, as I construe, comes of her greatness; it is because there is an Infinite in her, which with all her cunning she cannot quite bury under the Finite.

Let woman once overcome her selfish terror at her own finitude, and her finitude is, in one sense, overcome.

The mass of women lead lives of quiet desperation.

It's an ill wind that bloweth no woman to good.

Philosophy

A tear is worth a thousand smiles.

Women trust their ears less than their eyes.

She listens well who records on tape.

Every woman takes the limits of her own field of
vision for the limits of the world.

There are two sides to every question and lots of questions.

She who would distinguish the true from the false must
have an adequate idea of what is true and false.

Straight from the mare's mouth.

Tell her to live by yes and no - yes to everything good,
no to everything bad.

Woman is the only animal that eats when she is not
hungry, drinks when she is not thirsty, and makes love
at all seasons.

Bad women live that they may eat and drink, whereas
good women eat and drink that they may live.

Philosophy

Misery acquaints a woman with strange bedfellows.

No woman is happy who does not think herself so.

During her lifetime, an individual should devote her efforts to create happiness and to enjoy it, and also to keep it in store in society so that individuals of the future may also enjoy it.

A lifetime of happiness! No woman alive could bear it: it would be hell on earth.

The woman who lets herself be bored is even more contemptible than the bore.

It is almost a definition of a gentlewoman to say she is one who never inflicts pain.

No woman is justified in doing evil on the ground of expediency.

I forgot who it was that recommended women for their soul's good to do each day two things they disliked...it is a precept that I have followed scrupulously; for every day I have got up and I have gone to bed.

Philosophy

Early to bed and early to rise, makes a woman healthy, wealthy, and wise.

She that riseth late must trot all day.

This above all: to thine own self be true,
And it must follow, as night the day,
Thou canst not then be false to any woman.

Nothing astonishes women so much as common sense and plain dealing.

An honest woman's word is as good as her bond.

Would Diogenes have had better luck looking for an honest woman?

Mother, I cannot tell a lie, I did it with my little chain saw.

Every woman feels instinctively that all the beautiful sentiments in the world weigh less than a single lovely action.

She who praises everybody, praises nobody.

Philosophy

You can tell the character of every woman when you see how she receives praise.

She will hew to the line of right, let the chips fall where they may.

The more things a woman is ashamed of, the more respectable she is.

Trust that woman in nothing who has not a conscience in everything.

She flattered herself on being a woman without any prejudices; and this pretension itself is a very great prejudice.

A woman may love a paradox without either losing her wit or her honesty.

She who doesn't lose her wits over certain things has no wits to lose.

That immaculate womanliness we feel within ourselves, so far within us, that it remains intact though all the outer character seem gone; bleeds with keenest anguish at the undraped spectacle of a valor-ruined woman.

Philosophy

We live, but a world has passed away with the years that
perished to make us women.

She who laughs last, laughs best.

The science of life is a superb and dazzlingly lighted
hall which may be reached only by passing through
a long and ghastly kitchen.

Hickory dickory dock,
Two mice ran up the clock,
The clock struck one,
And the other one got away;
Hickory dickory dock.

You can't appreciate home till you've left it, money
till it's spent, your husband till he's joined a man's
club, nor Old Glory till you see it hanging on a
broomstick on the shanty of a consul in a foreign town.

Time waits for no woman.

Two maids that thought there was no more behind,
But such a day tomorrow as today,
And to be girl eternal.

Philosophy

She who is of a calm and happy nature will hardly feel the pressure of age, but to her who is of an opposite disposition youth and age are equally a burden.

To her whose elastic and vigorous thought keeps pace with the sun, the day is a perpetual morning.

Misspending a woman's time is a kind of self-homicide.

Young women think old women are fools; but old women know young women are fools.

A round woman cannot be expected to fit in a square hole right away. She must have time to modify her shape.

Time is the most valuable thing a woman can spend.

Every woman desires to live long, but no woman would be old.

No one is so old that she cannot live another year, nor so young that she cannot die today.

Philosophy

I would gladly give half of the beauty with which I am
credited for half of the wit you possess.

Is it true Non-Blondes have more un-fun? Be a Masochist
and see.

Beauty is in the eye of the holder of the bees.

The gardener Eve and her husband smile at the claims
of long descent.

The Fountain of Oldth.

When a woman fell into her anecdotage, it was a sign
for her to retire.

From forty till fifty a woman is at heart either a stoic
or a nymph.

We do not count a woman's years until she has nothing
else to count.

Book Title: How To Lose Friends And Influenzate People.

A woman is known by the company she keeps.

Philosophy

I never met a woman I didn't like.

A friend may well be reckoned the mistresspiece of Nature.

A woman's real life is that accorded to her in the thoughts
of other women by reason of respect or natural love.

In the life a young woman the most essential thing
for happiness is the gift of friendship.

O beautiful for spacious skies,
For amber waves of grain,
For purple mountain majesties
Above the fruited plain!
America! America!
Goddess shed her grace on thee
And crown thy good with sisterhood
From sea to shining sea!

What a chimera then is woman! What a novelty! What
a monster, what a chaos, what a contradiction, what a
prodigy! Judge of all things, feeble earthworm, depository
of truth, a sink of uncertainty and error, the glory and the
shame of the universe.

INDEPENDENCE

No woman is an island, entire of itself; every woman is a piece of the continent, a part of the main; if a clod be washed away by the sea, America is the less, as well as if a promontory were, as well as if a manor of thy friends or of thine own were; any woman's death diminishes me, because I am involved in womankind; and therefore never send to know for whom the bell tolls; it tolls for thee.

If a woman does not keep pace with her companions, perhaps it is beacuse she hears a different drummer. Let her step to the music she hears, however measured or far away.

Book Title: The Daughter Also Rises

I know of no more encouraging fact than the unquestionable ability of woman to elevate her life by conscious endeavor.

Whoso would be a woman must be a nonconformist.

To be a great woman and a saint for oneself, that is the one important thing.

Let each woman have the wit to go her own way.

I share no woman's opinions; I have my own.

Independence

In battle or business, whatever the game,
In law or love, it is ever the same;
In the struggle for power, or the scramble for pelf,
Let this be your motto - Rely on yourself!
For, whether the prize be a ribbon or throne,
The victor is she who can go it alone!

Every woman is the architect of her own fortune.

Do what thy womanhood bids thee do, from none but self
expect applause;
She noblest lives and noblest dies who makes and keeps
her self-made laws

Everybody likes and respects self-made women. It is
a great deal better to be made in that way than not to
be made at all.

Behind every successful woman is her *own* shadow.

A woman should *be* upright, not be *kept* upright.

The strongest woman in the world is she who stands
most alone.

The peculiarity of the New England hermit has not been

Independence

her desire to get near to Goddess, but her anxiety to get
away from woman.

Abandon ship! Every woman for herself!

The woman who goes alone can start today; but she who
travels with another must wait till that other is ready.

There can be no progress (real, that is, moral) except
in the individual and by the individual herself.

Woman: Mother thyself!

Every bitch has her day.

Are you a woman or a mouse?

That woman who lives for self alone
Lives for the meanest mortal known.

Be not thy sister's curator.

It was her peculiar doctrine that a woman has a perfect
right to interfere by force with the slaveholder, in order to

Independence

rescue the slave. I agree with her.

    The great woman is she who in the midst of the crowd keeps with perfect sweetness the independence of solitude.

    I never found the companion that was so companionable as solitude. We are for the most part more lonely when we go abroad among women than when we stay in our chambers. A woman thinking or working is always alone, let her be where she will.

    A wise woman never loses anything if she have herself.

    If you can't stand the heat, go back to the kitchen.

WORK I

I don't like work - no woman does - but I like what is in work - the chance to find yourself. Your own reality - for yourself, not for others - what no other woman can ever know.

This will separate the women from the girls.

The mistress word, work, is the open sesame to every portal, the great equalizer in the world, the true philosopher's stone which transmutes all the base metal of humanity into gold.

That power which erring women call Chance.

Labor disgraces no woman; unfortunately you occasionally find women disgrace labor.

In the morning, when thou art sluggish at rousing thee, let this thought be present: "I am rising to a woman's work."

It is not easy for women to rise whose qualities are thwarted by poverty.

Do not pray for easy lives. Pray to be stronger women! Do not pray for tasks equal to your power. Pray for powers equal to your tasks.

Work I

Work, and your house shall be duly fed;
Work, and rest shall be won;
I hold that a woman had better be dead
Than alive when her work is done.

Let each woman pass her days in that wherein her skill is greatest.

In the long run women hit only what they aim at.

Women of genius do not excel in any profession because they labor in it, but they labor in it because they excel.

Blessed is she who has found her work; let her ask no other blessedness.

Every woman loves what she is good at.

Work brings its own relief;
She who most idle is
Has most grief.

She that lives upon hope will die fasting.

Work I

For want of an innertube the tire is lost, for want of a
tire the car is lost, for want of a car the driver is lost.

She's not worth her salt.

No one knows what she can do till she tries.

Goddess made integers, all else is the work of women.

A really busy person neber knows how much she weighs.

An inability to stay quiet is one of the most conspicuous
failings of womankind.

She that has patience may compass anything.

Woman is so made that she can only find relaxation
from one kind of labor by taking up another.

No woman is really happy or safe without a hobby, and it
makes precious little difference what the outside interest
may be - botany, beetles or butterflies, roses, tulips or
irises; fishing, mountaineering or antiquities - anything
will do so long as she straddles a hobby and rides it hard.

Work I

'Tis not what woman does which exalts her, but what woman would do!

To be honest, to be kind - to earn a little and spend a little less, to make upon the whole a family happier for her presence, to renounce when that shall be necessary and not to be embittered, to keep a few friends, but there without capitulation - above all, on the same grim condition, to keep friends with herself - here is a task for all that a woman has of fortitude and delicacy.

WORK II

"If at first you don't succeed, try, try, again, "remarked
Goddess, removing Adam's rib.

Is it natural or womanmade?

Advice to a Young Tradeswoman: Remember that time
is money.

The youth gets together her materials to build a bridge to
the moon, or perchance, a palace or temple on earth, and
at length, the middle-aged woman concludes to build a
woodshed with them.

For 'tis sport to have the enginer hoist with her own petar.

She flies through the air with the greatest of ease,
The daring young woman on the flying trapeze.

The fate of the architect is the strangest of all. How often
she expends her whole soul, her whole heart and passion,
to produce buildings into which she may never enter.

Womankind was never so happily inspired as when it made a
cathedral.

Work II

Heroinic architecture.

A woman that has a taste of music, painting, or architecture, is like one that has another sense, when compared
with such as have no relish of those arts.

The critical sense is so far from frequent that it is
absolutely rare, and the possession of the cluster of
qualities that minister to it is one of the highest dis-
tinctions.... In this light one sees the critic as the real
helper of the artist, a torchbearing outrider, the interpreter, the sister.... Just in proportion as she is sentient
and restless, just in proportion as she reacts and recipro-
cates and penetrates, is the critic a valuable instrument.

She is the greatest artist who has embodied, in the sum
of her works, the greatest number of the greatest ideas.

The imitator is a poor kind of creature. If the woman
who paints only the tree, or flower, or other surface she
sees before her were an artist, the queen of artists would
be the photographer. It is for the artist to do something
beyond this: in portrait painting to put on canvas something more than the face the model wears for that one day;
to paint the woman, in short, as well as her features.

Art is a human activity having for its purpose the trans-
mission to others of the highest and best feelings to
which women have risen.

Work II

There was ease in Cassie's manner as she stepped into her place,
There was pride in Cassie's bearing, and a smile on Cassie's face,
And when, responding to the cheers, she lightly doffed her hat,
No stranger in the crowd could doubt 'twas Cassie at the bat.

Oh! somewhere in this favored land the sun is shining bright;
The band is playing somewhere, and somewhere hearts are light;
And somewhere gals are laughing and somewhere children shout,
But there is no joy in Mudville - mighty Cassie has struck out.

Go West, young woman.

The Owl and the Pussycat went to sea in a beautiful pea-green vessel for transport by water, constructed to provide bouyancy by excluding water and shaped to give stability and permit propulsion.

Workwomanship.

In a calm sea every woman is a pilot.

Work II

Midshipwoman.

Let the girl win her spurs.

You can set the trough before the horse, but you can't make her drink.

I'll resk forty dollars that she can out jump any frog in Calaveras county.

To own a bit of ground, to scratch it with a hoe, to plant seeds, and watch the renewal of life - this is the commonest delight of the race, the most satisfactory thing a woman can do.

Hiring on as a scarecrow fit her to a T.

What a woman needs in gardening is a cast-iron back, with a hinge in it.

You're a better woman than I am, Gunga Din.

Bye baby bunting
Mommy's gone a-hunting,
Gone to get a rabbit skin
To wrap the baby bunting in.

Work II

Book Title: The Woman In The Gray Flannel Suit

When I was a lass I served a term
As office girl to an Attorney's firm.
I cleaned the windows and I swept the floor
And I polished up the handle of the big front door.
I polished up that handle so carefullee
That now I am the Ruler of the Queen's Navee!

She uses language that would make your hair curl.
(She ought to take up barbering.)

The Businesswoman's haircut.

Workwoman's compensation insurance.

Perpetual devotion to what a woman calls her business,
is only to be sustained by perpetual neglect of many
other things.

The Businesswoman's lunch.

Is a potato chip a sin?

Necessity is the father of invention.

Work II

All work, even cotton-spinning, is noble.... A life of ease is not for any woman, nor for any goddess.

The twentieth century marked the rise of the merchant princess.

The greater philosopher a woman is, the more difficult it is for her to answer the foolish questions of common people.

She who can, does. She who cannot, teaches.

A teacher effects eternity; she can never tell where her influence stops.

A woman is not idle because she is absorbed in thought. There is a visible labor, and there is an invisible labor.

Clergywoman.

My definition of a philosopher is of a woman up in a balloon with her family and friends holding the ropes which confine her to the earth and trying to haul her down.

The Old Woman of the Mountain.

Work II

Women hang out their signs indicative of their respective trades: shoemakers hang out a gigantic shoe; jewelers a monster watch; and the dentist hangs out a gold tooth; but up in the mountains of New Hampshire, Goddess Almighty has hung out a sign to show that there She makes women.

Woman proposes, Goddess disposes.

The ugliest trades have their moments of pleasure. Now, if I were a grave digger, or even a hangwoman, there are some people I could work for with a great deal of enjoyment.

A zealous locksmith died of late,
And did arrive at heaven gate,
She stood without and would not knock,
Because she meant to pick the lock.

LIFE AND DEATH

In the beginning Goddess created the heaven and the earth.

And the earth was without form, and void; and darkness was upon the face of the deep. And the Spirit of Goddess moved upon the face of the waters.

And Goddess said, Let there be light: and there was light.

And Goddess saw that it was good.

And Goddess said, Let us make woman in our own image, after our likeness.

And Goddess formed woman of the dust of the ground, and breathed into her nostrils the breath of life; and woman became a living soul.

I am that which began;
Out of me the years roll;
Out of me Goddess and woman;
I am equal and whole;
Goddess changes, and woman, and the form of them bodily; I am the soul.

The New Testament, and to a very large extent the Old, *is* the soul of woman. You cannot criiticize it. It criticizes you.

Life And Death

The soul of woman is larger than the sky, deeper than the oceans, or the abysmal dark of the unfathomed center.

The soul of woman is immortal and imperishable.

It is not good that the woman should be alone; I will make her an 'elp meet for her.

And the rib, which Goddess had taken from woman made she a man.

And they were both naked, the woman and her husband, and they were not ashamed.

To give the devil her due.

Each of us bears her own Hell.

Sickness, sin and death being inharmonious, do not originate in Goddess nor belong to Her government.

The heart of woman is the place the devils dwell in: I feel sometimes a hell within myself.

Life And Death

The Princess of Darkness.

Your eyes shall be opened, and ye shall be as goddesses, knowing good and evil.

The man whom thou gavest to be with me, he gave me of the tree and I did eat.

What is this that thou hast done? And the man said, The serpent beguiled me, and I did eat.

The belief in a supernatural source of evil is not necessary; women alone are quite capable of every wickedness.

If a woman have a strong faith she can indulge in the luxury of skepticism.

There is no steady unretracing progress in this life; we do not advance through fixed gradations, and at the last one pause: through infancy's unconscious spell, girlhood's thoughtless faith, adolescence' doubt (the common doom), then skepticism, then disbelief, resting at last in womanhood's pondering repose of If. But once gone through, we trace the round again; and are infants, girls, and women and Ifs eternally. Where lies the final harbor, whence we unmoor no more?

Life And Death

Religion is a woman's total reaction upon life.

She has defiled her mother's grave.

One woman's religion neither harms nor helps another woman.

Religion is a great force - the only real motive force in the world; but what you fellows don't understand is that you must get at a woman through her own religion and not through yours.

What is it: is woman only a blunder of Goddess, or Goddess only a blunder of woman?

The great act of faith is when woman decides that she is not Goddess.

At bottom Goddess is nothing more than an exalted mother.

Turn over a new belief.

Is Goddess dead?

Life And Death

Women reject their prophets and slay them, but they love their martyrs and honor those whom they have slain.

If Goddess did not exist, it would be necessary to invent Her.

Every woman is her own doctor of divinity, in the last resort.

Blessed be she that cometh in the name of the Lady.

Follow me, and I will make you fishers of women.

The Lady is my shepherdess; I shall not want.

A woman that'd expict to thrain lobsters to fly in a year is called a loonytic; but a woman that thinks women can be tu-urned into angels be an iliction is called a rayformer an' remains at large.

Surely goodness and mercy shall follow me all the days of my life: and I will live in the house of the Lady for ever.

The way of Heaven has no favorites. It is always with the good woman.

Life And Death

How good is woman's life, the mere living! now fit to employ
All the heart and soul and the senses forever in joy!

Our mother which art in heaven, hallowed be thy name.
Thy queendom come. Thy will be done on earth, as it is in
heaven. Give us this day our daily bread. And forgive us
our trespasses, as we forgive those who trespass against us.
And lead us not into temptation, but deliver us from evil:
for thine is the queendom, and the power, and the glory,
for ever. Awomen.

Who rises from prayer a better woman, her prayer is answered.

Four things are necessary for the salvation of woman:
to know what she ought to believe; to know what she
ought to desire; to know what she ought to do; and to
act upon this knowledge.

From ghoulies and ghosties and longleggety beasties
And things that go bump in the night, Good Lady
deliver us!

She could open either door she pleased.... If she opened
the one, there came out of it a hungry tiger, the fiercest
and most cruel that could be procured, which immediately
sprang upon her, and tore her to pieces, as a punishment for her
guilt.... But if the accused person opened the other door, there
came forth from it a gentleman, the most suitable to her
years and station.... So I leave it with all of you: Which

Life And Death

came out of the open door - the gentleman or the tiger?

Now I lay me down to sleep,
I pray the Lady my soul to keep;
If I should die before I wake,
I pray the Lady my soul to take.

Most women eddy about
Here and there, eat and drink,
Chatter and love and hate,
Gather and squander, are raised
Aloft, are hurled in the dust,
Striving blindly, achieving
Nothing; and then they die.

Woman came I out of my mother's womb, and woman
shall I return thither.

Opera Title: The Flying Dutchwoman

Death is afraid of her because she has the heart of a lioness.

Woman: giveth up the ghost.

Goddess Save The Queen!

Life And Death

The Lady giveth and the Lady taketh away. Blessed be the name of the Lady.

Thou anointest my flat-head six with oil; my odometer runneth over.

Every woman meets her Waterloo at last.

She hath awakened from the dream of life.

Friends, Americans, countrywomen, lend me your ears.

Her life was gentle, and the elements so mix'd in her that Nature might stand up and say to all the world, "This was a woman!"

The soil out of which such women as she are made is good to be born on, good to live on, good to die for and to be buried in.

She was a woman, take her all in all,
I shall not look upon her like again.

She that dies pays all debts.

The one who goes is happier
Than those she leaves behind.

Life And Death

Truth sits upon the lips of dying women.

When a woman is dead, they put money in her coffin, erect monuments to her memory, and celebrate the anniversary of her birthday in set speeches. Would they take notice of her if she were living? No!

Blest be the woman that spares these stones,
And curst be she that moves my bones.

As for a future life, every woman must judge for herself between conflicting vague probabilities.

I leave eternity to Thee; for what is woman that she should live out the lifetime of her Goddess?

The prophesying business is like writing fugues; it is fatal to everyone save the woman of genius.

Because I could not stop for Death,
She kndly stopped for me -
The Carriage held but just Ourselves
And Immortality.